THE PSALMS OF BABYLON

Or, 112 Flowers Of Malaise

G.R. TOMAINI

978-0-6456700-8-0

The Psalms Of Babylon:
Or, 112 Flowers Of Malaise

G.R. Tomaini

© Indigo Dragon, Melbourne, Australia, 2023.

All rights reserved, no section of this book may be utilized without permission, except brief quotations, including electronic reproductions without the permission of the copyright holders and publisher. Published in Australia.

Thema Classification: DCF (Poetry).

MANTICORE PRESS
WWW.MANTICORE.PRESS

For:

    Charles Baudelaire
    Wallace Stevens
    Jacques Derrida
    Jacques Lacan
    Avital Ronell
    Jean Matthee
    Linda Stern
    David Katz
    John Foy
    Sharone
    Mitchell
    Uday
    Andrew
    Ivan
    Chander
    Gary Carter
    The Wily and Handsome Sir Christopher Leake
    Gwendolyn Taunton
    Parvathy Salil, my brilliant friend from London
    & The Morningside Poetry Series Poets

CONTENTS

Preface 11

1. *Asphyxiation; Jouissance!* 15
2. *Sedimented Toad:* 16
   Unrequited Love
3. *Ragnarok:* 17
   Tummy Rub
4. *Infinite Absolution* 18
5. *Sinning Grace* 20
6. *Phony:* 21
   Cacophony
7. *Unholy Family:* 22
   Pedigree Of The Damned
8. *Bleach Bath:* 24
   Confession
9. *Dejected:* 25
   Not Dead
10. *Lacoön:* 26
    Serpents Of Love
11. *Rueful Rotting* 28
12. *Checkmated Soul* 29
13. *Laureled Sinner:* 30

Excelsior

14. Sin And Surf: 32
    Kowabunga
15. Gorge Of The Grass Fed Geese 33
16. Lascivious Inquiries: 34
    Asking After Your Soul
17. Moral Luck: 36
    Spontaneous Combustion
18. Tomb Of A Libertine 37
19. Grandfather Clock: 38
    Lament
20. Descent Into Hell 40
21. Monsoon: 41
    Sea Shanty Tune
22. Poltergeist: 42
    Of Love
23. Concrete Ballet Shoes 44
24. Marooned: 45
    In An Opium Den
25. One Has A Life: 46
    Procure One A Cig
26. Dark Metanoia 48
27. Soliloquy Of The Moon 49
28. Cauterized Soul: 50
    Festering Wound: Empty Womb
29. Coffin Clothes 52
30. Whatever Forever Means 53
31. Cognoscenti Of Souls 54
32. Silent Night 57
33. Disciples of Keatsian-Sadism 58
34. Crucifixion Of The Rose 59
35. The Cock Has Come Home To Roost 61

36. Deplorable Sins: 62
    Sinnerbabe
37. Creature In The Attic 63
38. Talk To The Hand: 66
    The Hand Of Death
39. Never Forget: 67
    Never Forgive
40. Beneath The Earthen Mud 68
41. Gunpowder: 70
    Soul: Flame
42. Times Square: 71
    Stirs Of Life
43. Hung In The Snow 72
44. Duck Duck Goose 74
45. Noxious Perfume 75
46. Science Fair Project 76
47. Merry Go Round 78
48. Behind The Roses 79
49. Waterboarders Of Soul 80
50. Butterfly Wings 82
51. Tarantulan Souls 83
52. Besmitten: 84
    In The Belly Of Lady Dread
53. Nutcracker Waltz 85
54. Worn Out Soles 86
55. Sour Milk: 87
    Sullen Dreams: Capricious Lies
56. American Malaise 88
57. Prudential Sin 89
58. Barbed Wire Chrysalis 90
59. Ashes To Ashes 92
60. Soul Running Cold: 93
    Pneumonia

61. Unholy Grins: 94
    Respectable Sins
62. Heartbreaker 95
63. Cookie Cutter Sadists... 96
64. Mommy Mummy: 97
    Tomb In The Womb
65. Suddenly A Tramp 99
66. Lobotomized Soul..100
67. Salacious Siren: 101
    Whispers Of The Conch Shell
68. Abandoned: 103
    Hymn To Jealousy
69. Too Cool For School 104
70. Medusa Gaze:... 105
    Kiss Of The Razor Blade
71. Banal Souls...107
72. Set Sail: 108
    Malaise
73. Saturnine Lover:..109
    Incubated Soul
74. Necromancer: 110
    Capitalist
75. Atonement: 111
    Miami Bleach
76. Pried Open Clam: 112
    Rose Golden Sarcophagus: Ragdoll Toy
77. One's Miss Angeline..113
78. World's Shortest Novel..................................... 114
79. Parrot Of Doom: 115
    Dark Instructions
80. Brooklyn Banshee...117
81. Sins Of The Flesh 118
82. Bathtub Maelstrom: 119

Oasis In The Sewer

83. Forces Of Assholedom 120
84. Balm Requested: 121
    Balm Denied
85. Moral Tax Evasion: 122
    Defense Of The Pious Sin
86. Only Time May Tell... 123
87. Bedwetting Soul:...124
    Bleach Is A Cure-All
88. Soul Craters: 125
    Operas On The Moon
89. Blue Skies And Golden Sunshine...................... 126
90. Octopus:... 127
    Suction Cups To The Soul
91. Desperate Seance:..128
    Morning Of The Mourning
92. Wanton Souls: 129
    Hide In The Dark
93. Desirous To Die 130
94. Pop: 131
    Up On A Hot Air Balloon
95. Soul Harpoon: 132
    Bad Luck Opal
96. One's Tender Buttons 133
97. Hymn To Gluttony: 134
    Hymn To Decadence
98. Hounds Of Hell.. 136
99. Sunflower Versus Wrecking Ball....................... 137
100. Barricade: 138
    Battering Ram: Soul Dons A White Flag
101. Soul In The Trough:.. 139
    Hungry Hogs
102. Aloha From The Void..140

103. Easter Clothes: 141
    Woodchipper Of Souls: Jigsaw Puzzle

104. Methinks One Loves You 142

105. Bore Some More: 143
    Increased Ennui

106. Shock Treatment: 144
    Soul Transfusion: Cure For Banality

107. Your Legs: 146
    A Deceptive Trap

108. Fortune Cookie: 147
    The Black Spot

109. Hall Of Mirrors: 148
    Malaise

110. Laughing Gas 150

111. All Roads Lead To Hell 151

112. Baby's First Word: 152
    Tequila

PREFACE

In the realm of words and wanderings, I present a tapestry woven with threads of dedication to the specters of Charles Baudelaire, Edgar Allen Poe, Franz Kafka, Sylvia Plath, and Emily Dickinson. I offer up these Psalms that sing of truth and paradox. Baudelaire loves them; he told me as much when I hosted a seance to conjure up his decadent soul from the depths of Hell. He told me to pray *harder*, particularly for one aspiration: Insurmountable Victory. So I did and was blessed with boon after boon… wound after wound…; alas, no one knows quite like your author what it means to bask in the light of the blackest possible Sun: Victory over and above one's insipid nemeses.

This tome is also offered to my lovers, those who have graced my life without whom I am: a meandering soul lost somewhere in between his personal harem of doe-eyed Brooklyn twinks and the enigma of insufferable garçons.

In the corridors of desire, no amount of cougar dominatrices could console my battered blood pumper, for it is a heart that knows the waterboard, woodchipper, and the asphyxiation of *jouissance*, both obscene and officious.

Like a Confucian gentleman, polished with elevated mores and refined etiquette, I journey as *Il Maestro*, engaging in a reconstruction of philosophy through psycho-philosophical poems that delve into the depths of the dark soul and the debris of social detritus.

In this collection, I offer wicked poems that embrace the lascivious, licentious, and salacious nature of existence, for I am voracious in my exploration of ideology and ideological warfare.

As I emerge from my barbed wire chrysalis, I reflect on the ontological status of the strip club lunch special, all of the deplorable hearts that I've cannibalized in love, and the naivety of charm itself. I am a vigorous lover, dwelling in a modest villa on the outskirts of Milan, unbothered by accusations of an essence and nature most Eurotrash, indeed.

When Gwendolyn Taunton said she would put the whore of Babylon on the cover of the *Psalms*, I thought she was speaking of me, referred to by some as an *enfant* terrible of the humanities. However, I liken myself more to a Caesar who crossed the Rubicon of German Idealism, never to look back again…

Babylon, dashed against the rocks, embodies hopes and dreams, and within its confines lies the elusive definition of malaise. With *soppressata* gout and my dandy pimp cane, I contemplate fitting in with the Oxford sodomites. *How I am a provincial philistine in the streets, but a libertine in the sheets!*

Oh, Svengali! Oh, Trilby! — a dance of manipulation and allure that I navigate as Prey for Superpredators, recalling that I was almost a male stripper — a chapter in a life filled with poetic audacity. When harangued by those who would bark: "Your text is almost as egregious as your own patsy ass," one can merely riposte: *"Ich bin Gucci Guilty!"*

Until Next I Win—,
The I That Is We, The We That Is I—,

Oh, Puccini!—,

Auf Wiedersehen—,

Il Maestro—,
The Prince of Dialectics—,

Signore G.R. Tomaini

1. ASPHYXIATION; JOUISSANCE!

I

On Calvary: He Hangs:
Nailed to the Wood: *the Lamb!*
God in Heaven sat Upright:
Eyes Fixated on *Jesus Baby* ...

II

God Said: *Slow Time!*
Play that Part Again,
when the Spear Pierces!
'Tis Ecstasy, to see Him Suffer!

III

He Inches toward Death:
Angels get him *Vinegar*!
One True Son: Hung:
Asphyxiated: *Oh the Jouissance!*

2. SEDIMENTED TOAD: UNREQUITED LOVE

Sedimented Toad:
Frigid: Frozen Under Ice!
Does Your Heart Still Beat?

3. RAGNAROK: TUMMY RUB

Now the World Must Burn:
Beforehand: just one Small Ask:
Spare a Tummy Rub?

4. INFINITE ABSOLUTION

I

> Bells atop the Cathedral Ring:
> Drop One off out Front:
> Sin-Stained to One's Core!

II

> Get out of One's Way, Pastor!
> Where is the Juice Kept?
> They call it Infinite Absolution ...

III

> Here it is: Glug, Glug, Glug ...
> Euphoria: One's Soul is Bleachy Clean!
> Against Sin One is Vaccinated!

IV

> More Infinite Absolution!
> On it One Must Imbibe ...
> One Hears a Rumbling Noise ...

V

Ah! Infinite Absolution:
it is Bursting in through the Windows!
One can Sin and Sin and Sin!

VI

One's Soul is Swollen:
Drunk on Infinite Absolution ...
a Blank Check Signed by Jesus Christ!

5. SINNING GRACE

Salvific Dogma:
One Can Sin and Be Saved, too!
One's Creed: Sinning Grace!

6. PHONY: CACOPHONY

Soul Cacophony:
Making lots of Noise; Truth is:
your Soul is Phony!

7. UNHOLY FAMILY: PEDIGREE OF THE DAMNED

I

Herein lies:
G.R. Tomaini:
Pallbearer of:
American Malaise.

II

Pedigree of the Damned:
Charles Baudelaire: Father!
Arthur Rimbaud: Uncle!
Sylvia Plath: Sister!

III

Franz Kafka: Brother!
Anne Sexton: Sister!
Edgar Allen Poe: Grandfather!
Emily Dickinson: Grandmother!

IV

Composers prepare a tune:
to capture all the Malaise:
that orbits about their poetry;
there is no Shelter for the Soul!

8. BLEACH BATH: CONFESSION

Confess your Sins, now!
Bleach your Soul: Saith the Priest!
Scrub Brush all its Stains!

9. DEJECTED: NOT DEAD

One Sits in the Dark:
Alone: Humiliated:
Dejected: not Dead ...

10. LAOCOÖN: SERPENTS OF LOVE

I

Pardon: one is Ensnared:
by Serpents of Love: hiss!
One shall introduce you:
below are one's Favorites!

II

Banality — ubiquitous ideal:
precondition for Sin: Soul?
A Banal Soul is formable:
so many things to be: to try!

III

Decadence — stems from Banality:
one over indulges after:
a period of Banal restraint:
followed by Avalanches of Sin!

IV

Ennui — begins just when:
Decadent thrills Wilt into Nothing:
numbness of the Soul prevails:
but one grows bored: with boredom!

V

Malaise — vilest of all:
yet a sweet Love, nevertheless;
to be Malaised is to Breathe:
the Air of the Living Dead!

VI

Lacoön: Exemplar of a Universal Plight:
Serpents of Love consume you:
just as do they Asphyxiate: our
Vulnerable Souls: Sitting Ducks!

11. RUEFUL ROTTING

Under the Soil:
the Rueful Rotting Occurs;
Souls Taken too Soon ...

12. CHECKMATED SOUL

Your Soul to E Five:
one's Castle to E Six:
Your Soul: Checkmated!

13. LAURELED SINNER: EXCELSIOR

I

Night — especially in the Night —
and Day: you commit Sin!

II

Accolades? Sinner has many:
how you are Virtuous to the Dark!

III

Nevermore consider the Light:
Another trophy! Another medal!

IV

Laureled Sinner: Relentless:
you pursue Evil for its own Sake!

V

Your Motto: Excelsior!
Your Praxis: Excelsior!

VI

Restless in your Vocation:
Sin calls: back to work!

14. SIN AND SURF: KOWABUNGA

So how are the Waves?
Surfing for the Sake of Sin:
Kowabunga, Dude!

15. GORGE OF THE GRASS FED GEESE

Their Meal: your Soul: Diced;
Watching the Grass Fed Geese Gorge:
was Gratifying ...

16. LASCIVIOUS INQUIRIES: ASKING AFTER YOUR SOUL

I

> Wonder: where was your Soul:
> as the Hounds of Hell raised?

II

> Wonder: how was your Soul doing:
> after all those Bellicose Conflicts?

III

> Wonder: what was the Time:
> when your Soul Popped its Cherry?

IV

> Wonder: was your Soul Good:
> across your Festivals of Decadence?

V

Wonder: what happens to your Soul:
when the Malaise Overtakes it ?

VI

Sweet scent of your Malaise:
Truffle Pigs Inhale it Gaily!

17. MORAL LUCK: SPONTANEOUS COMBUSTION

Luck is on one's Side:
Spontaneous Combustion:
may Occur Today!

18. TOMB OF A LIBERTINE

Last Act: Sent Flowers;
from the Grave he Leers at you:
Asleep in one's Arms ...

19. GRANDFATHER CLOCK: LAMENT

Only just then, then never more:
ding goes the chime, alert, alert!

Incoming devastation, a heart races:
in time , one will see, what every hour

haunts one, each ring, each ding:
forever more rattles one; the gong ...

shatters a peace of Mind, can one —
resonate with a Grandfather Clock,

ding it goes, spun in delicate cycles,
gears humming in and throughout:

Clock, o Clock, on a deathbed one ...
sat consigned, waiting for one final ...

pronouncement: a Clock bet with the ...
house; a metric for one's damnation:

then the Clock died on one before —
one died on the Grandfather Clock;

nailed with each passing second,
woven — more like — perhaps stitched:

all is well here, please go; one has ...
beaten out the Clock, what is this ?

A new Grandfather Clock: still is one —
grandfathered in, secured as it were ,

from any opportunity for escape: no ...
absence from impending devastation!

One thought one had conquered time:
one thought, one erred, then one died.

From the abyss one understands:
it is all Despair! Ennui! Malaise!

20. DESCENT INTO HELL

Further one Descends;
down here not one Understands:
what Being in Love Means ...

21. MONSOON: SEA SHANTY TUNE

The Forecast: Monsoon!
Heave! Ho! Board up the Windows!
A Sea Shanty Tune ...

22. POLTERGEIST: OF LOVE

On a cold Winter night I brought you ...
flowers — beautiful to behold — and yet:

when I ballooned into the room, I saw:
unconscious you, lying there, gone:

therein did I wilt, my brood released:
how, if, when, or for what purpose?

When the time comes I ring the police:
as my beauty is ushered away, I know

never will I excite again their beating —
heart, now all remains to be done:

is appease the ghost, active already;
you never grant me leave or rest:

until I am dead, you haunt me daily:
together, my love, we live my life,

until today, that is: the exorcist is ...
called, robed, and on his way:

ectoplasm encourages no fear in the —
Soul of the exorcist: say farewell:

to your haunted victim: to me: to I;
go now in peace, fly off into the void:

for, I bought you flowers: I bought —
you flowers, then you went and died;

have some courtesy, do show some —
respect: give up this gambit, join with —

the others of your kind, Specters,
Banshees, and Ghouls: I will never

forgive you: for I bought you flowers:
then you died: elephant in the room:

you will never understand how I feel:
you will never understand anything,

at all, ever again now are you truly ...
afield from my embrace: toodles it is!

The monster was thus cast out; too ...
bad for all of the Souls involved:

now there is only one person living —
this life, the specter is ostracized:

good grief, how I miss it! and yet ...
how I feel myself finally unshackled!

23. CONCRETE BALLET SHOES

You Ballerina —
are those Concrete Ballet Shoes?
Come out of the Sea!

24. MAROONED: IN AN OPIUM DEN

One's Last Breath Draws Near:
One: in an Opium Den:
Cries out for Dear Life!

25. ONE HAS A LIFE: PROCURE ONE A CIG

You must believe that from the night ...
before, one remains absolutely annihilated:

there is no monitor in sight, lighthouse ...
is probably shut down for a cig break;

if they are taking time to enjoy one,
one may as well join in too, because —

without a jumpstart, this state will last ...
forever and a day; be a good chum:

procure one a cig; watch one's troubles —
melt away, and the life return to one's ...

bones, and the grief pack up and go —
afar; today! Today! The cig rescues —

and delivers — from all, including those ...
who would destroy one's own Soul:

no more Kierkegaardian worries! Can ...
you see how a cigarette castles one ...

against one's maudlin frights? Now:
one has a life! A life! What shall one spend ...

it on, friends and nemeses, moon and ...
sun, stars and planets: one has a life:

One thinks one'll spend it on whatever one ...
damn well pleases; and another pack of cigs!

26. DARK METANOIA

Inside the Cocoon:
Light is Concealed in the Dark;
a Work in Progress!

27. SOLILOQUY OF THE MOON

All Will Betray You!
Listen to the Moon: Beware!
Malaise is Coming!

28. CAUTERIZED SOUL: FESTERING WOUND: EMPTY WOMB

I

One is in volcanic trouble:
womb wounds fester, deep;
needle and thread are useless:
take fire to the open gash!

II

Otherwise, it shall not Heal ...
One must swallow whole ...
the cautery iron: gulp!
Now one's Soul is warmed.

III

Death is certain, sure:
commandeer your strength:
next the doctor recommends:
that one gobble up the Sun!

IV

Then one will never be cold:
immune, for once, to arctic winds;
one resists a brutal truth:
nevermore will one adorn a womb.

29. COFFIN CLOTHES

Wear your Coffin Clothes:
which Day is a Mystery:
yet each Holds Promise ...

30. WHATEVER FOREVER MEANS

Love you Forever:
Whatever Forever Means:
to the Timekeeper ...

31. COGNOSCENTI OF SOULS

I

One has ensnared your ...
Soul: what ought one do?
One has many choices,
many options one could take ...

II

There are many paths, here:
some would make you happy,
others might lessen your pride;
one or two could break your heart ...

III

One now possesses your Soul:
ought one brandish the thing —
like a shiny brooch — or , toss it —
into a sea of salt — farewell!

IV

Or not ... one cannot ...
discern such a decision on ...
an empty stomach ... ah!
One shall feast upon your Soul!

V

You are bland and molden:
you tasteless bore! Your ...
Soul was unpeppered:
nevertheless one ate it ...

VI

You should thank one —
for gorging on your Soul:
the privilege was all yours;
you have nothing else to give!

VII

One has no use for you,
anymore: pack up your bags:
evict yourself out of one's life:
begone: leave one be: get!

THE PSALMS OF BABYLON

VIII

Still around? One will ...
do you a favor: one has —
fashioned a new Soul for you:
hollow once, now again whole!

IX

Oops, one has been tempted:
a Soul of one's own design:
yummy! Tastes better this time!
Ciao! More Souls to devour!

32. SILENT NIGHT

Ah: a Silent Night!
On a Nuclear Wasteland Site:
here there is no Life ...

33. DISCIPLES OF KEATSIAN-SADISM

Watch as they Pass by:
Disciples of Keats and Sade ;
Evil is Beauty!

34. CRUCIFIXION OF THE ROSE

I

One sent you a rose:
therein one erred —
now one is in despair:
hair falling out, weeping ...

II

One arrived at home:
one opened the mailbox:
what had you done! No!
A symbol of one's love defiled!

III

What rose deserved that:
to be nailed to a block:
one imagines the rose wept:
as you crucified it dead!

IV

> In that act you did one in:
> your poetic barb cut too deep —
> now one can say in earnest:
> that rose died for one's sins!

35. THE COCK HAS COME HOME TO ROOST

Your Attention, Please!
The Cock Has Come Home To Roost!
He Roosts in Malaise!

36. DEPLORABLE SINS: SINNERBABE

You know you have them:
Deplorable Sins; Golly!
What a Sinnerbabe!

37. CREATURE IN THE ATTIC

I

There one sat: in blackness;
over on the bed, lies you:
naked and inviting, and yet:
Creature in the Attic withholds!

II

Precious moment over dinner:
ensconced in darkness,
one will never experience it:
shipwrecked here in the attic!

III

One knows what one did —
and did not do: to you;
one is the Creature in the Attic:
a troubling memory, half-forgotten!

IV

> Creature in the Attic knows one thing:
> its place — alone — in purgatory;
> there is no balm for its condition:
> Creature in the Attic is doomed!

V

> Creature in the Attic is only:
> a figment of the imagination:
> never allow it a true existence:
> Creature in the Attic does not exist!

VI

> Creature in the Attic is:
> opposite you at the bar:
> one must be apathetic to it;
> or else it may linger!

VII

> Shoo, Creature! Go back
> to your Attic, stay there!
> Creature is not allowed outdoors:
> one apologizes for its behavior!

VIII

Mother pities the attic Creature:
one tells her to be strong:
the Creature is our burden:
not a toy, but a source of grief!

IX

Now the Creature gives birth:
its offspring are poems:
inspired by little old you:
how the Creature adores you!

X

Throw popcorn to the Creature:
watch it eat; soon the
harvest will come, and:
we shall cook the Creature!

XI

Into the boiling pot:
went the Creature: a martyr:
come, then, get your portion:
poet's heart: in a fine gravy!

38. TALK TO THE HAND: THE HAND OF DEATH

You: Talk to the Hand:
the Hand of Death: he Seeks You!
Collecting a Debt?

39. NEVER FORGET: NEVER FORGIVE

Say: Never Forget:
Never Forgive; one's Motto ...
Best you wrote it down!

40. BENEATH THE EARTHEN MUD

I

One simple prank should ...
do the brat good: grab ...
the shovel and the coffin:
call it a birthday surprise!

II

Run boy, run! Faster!
Caught: they took hold of him:
put him in the box: nailed it:
underground with dirt on top.

III

Mommy said: where is he?
Dawdling: is it supper time?
Rain began to fall: heavy:
hours flew by: nothing amiss.

IV

We forgot about him:
drowned in the earthen mud:
our brother: buried and gone!
Who will get his birthday presents?

V

Bang went the door:
eerie moaning out front:
I made a pact and am intact:
nevermind with who: ah, brothers!

VI

How your prank was so wise!
Now I will prank you forever:
gaze into my pupils, black:
leer in and see your future!

41. GUNPOWDER: SOUL: FLAME

Gunpowder: Soul: Flame;
The Match you Lit: one's whole Soul:
Implosion of Soul!

42. TIMES SQUARE: STIRS OF LIFE

Everyone: Malaised;
Stirs of Life: the Rats at least ...
possess Souls ... for now!

43. HUNG IN THE SNOW

I

Hail pelts the face:
icicles hit the head:
it raises an umbrella:
frost coats its fingers!

II

A sedimented toad:
under a layer of frozen pond:
so it is, to love you:
an umbrella fails to shelter!

III

A dentist's drill in the:
middle of a snow storm:
succubus of love: do it again:
abandon one for dead!

IV

Frozen face, frozen Soul:
frost upon the Soul, indeed:
stood up upon the stool:
kicked it loose: hung in the snow!

44. DUCK DUCK GOOSE

Let's play: Duck, Duck, Goose!
Running for one's very life:
Running from Malaise!

45. NOXIOUS PERFUME

Just the Scent of you:
Inhaling your Pheromones:
one Feels Malaised Joy!

46. SCIENCE FAIR PROJECT

I

> Take hold of the teenager:
> get him to sign consent:
> to participate in the experiment:
> tears shall be wrung out!

II

> Give him an empty room:
> there for two weeks keep:
> the door locked, him inside:
> ignore not the weeping: film it!

III

> Procure his most beloved:
> relatives, friends, and lovers:
> they will reveal to him that:
> him they despise with a passion!

IV

Put the subject on a stage:
how the spectators are amazed:
he was milked for scientific data:
but you won the Science Fair Prize!

47. MERRY GO ROUND

Round and Round one Goes:
a Free Act is a Fiction:
Cyclical ... is Soul!

48. BEHIND THE ROSES

One awaits the Call:
Ring! Must be that time of Day:
Malaise is here: Yay!

49. WATERBOARDERS OF SOUL

I

Glug, glug, glug:
another shot of Whiskey:
but not before the Wine:
poor Soul, weather this, once more!

II

A Soul drowned in liquor:
foie gras duck, but with Whiskey:
do a dance and do a hop:
Cirrhosis of the Soul looms!

III

Brave it out, once more:
good Soul, endangered, now:
a chorus of banshees calls out:
join us in the Realm of Spirits!

IV

Nay — one's Soul already ...
dwells in the Realm of Spirits:
Brandy, Sherry, and Absinthe;
funny joke: now you drown!

V

Cheers to you: who wished one dead:
gone out of sight forever:
empty hearts! Waterboarders of Soul!
Grant one this: one final drink!

50. BUTTERFLY WINGS

Did you cry when they:
pinned down your Butterfly Wings?
How you used to fly!

51. TARANTULAN SOULS

Tarantulan Souls:
Web Spinning like Arachnids;
be careful: they bite!

52. BESMITTEN: IN THE BELLY OF LADY DREAD

I

Remove, now, all of your clothes:
behold: Our Lady of Dread!

II

Next in line: time to be devoured:
close one's eyes: better off that way!

III

In the belly of Lady Dread:
besmitten, as she digests one!

IV

Her acid vanquishes one's Soul:
one's last words: Hail Lady Dread!

53. NUTCRACKER WALTZ

Drunken Nutcrackers:
fresh spin on Classic Ballet:
vomit on the stage ...

54. WORN OUT SOLES

One has worn out soles!
From walking all over Souls:
one sticks to one's shoe!

55. SOUR MILK: SULLEN DREAMS: CAPRICIOUS LIES

I

Abreast the teat: sour milk:
a rot deep in the Soul;
nursed on rancid milk:
ostracized from out the womb!

II

Sullen dreams in the night:
cool despondency in the day:
wipe away one's tears:
years — that way — become dreams!

III

Years spent within a dream:
howling at the Moon yields no good:
brave lies: whispers in the wind:
capricious liar: roast in Hell!

56. AMERICAN MALAISE

Red: White: Blue: Malaise:
an urge: Soul Detonation:
Malaise Wins the day!

57. PRUDENTIAL SIN

The Prudential Sin:
teach a Man how to do it:
he will Sin for life!

58. BARBED WIRE CHRYSALIS

I

Naptime begins:
so does a nightmare:
enter hopelessness:
enter despair!

II

Chrysalis:
shut up against:
all kinds of light:
darkness engulfs!

III

Wombed in wire:
twirled in a gyre:
ubiquitous silken slices:
wound after wound!

IV

Barbed wire:
wrapped around:
one's Soul: strangled ...
within the chrysalis ...

59. ASHES TO ASHES

Crematorium:
that is where one wants to be:
Ashes to Ashes!

60. SOUL RUNNING COLD: PNEUMONIA

Pardon: one's Soul runs Cold:
somebody gave one Pneumonia:
probably was you!

61. UNHOLY GRINS: RESPECTABLE SINS

I

Purple gloom: smiles:
false assurances of love:
no caring or kindness:
beneath your jackal eyes!

II

Complete your transaction:
you possess expensive tastes:
in Sin: you are respectable:
you teach at Sunday School!

III

You make one sick:
with your Unholy Grins:
you are not that slick:
Oil drips from your Greasy Soul!

62. HEARTBREAKER

Broke up two marriages;
sacred unions defiled:
wicked ones smiled!

63. COOKIE CUTTER SADISTS

The funny thing is:
you think you're real Sadists;
too Cookie Cutter!

64. MOMMY MUMMY: TOMB IN THE WOMB

I

Wombed in: a fetus:
in a mummified cadaver.

II

Lingering heartbeat:
they assumed you dead!

III

Fetal claws not sharp enough:
Mommy Mummy cannot help.

IV

Trapped: how quickly:
does womb become tomb!

V

> Cease to struggle, youngling:
> let this womb be your tomb!

VI

> Birth is a suicide mission:
> not one of us escapes Death!

VII

> Thus was your womb your tomb:
> are not you placated?

65. SUDDENLY A TRAMP

When your Luck runs out:
cash gone: hard fact to face: one's:
suddenly a Tramp!

66. LOBOTOMIZED SOUL

Lobotomized Soul;
Surgeon Left just enough Brain:
to still be Malaised!

67. SALACIOUS SIREN: WHISPERS OF THE CONCH SHELL

I

Ear pressed to the shell:
concentrated on the wind:
subtle whispers come through:
rip tide of the Soul!

II

Come into the Sea:
under the Waves one resides:
walk out: join with the Ocean:
forget your attachments: wade in!

III

Pull yourself together:
for, this is no time to drown:
now who will play with one?
Time to net another Soul!

IV

>Salacious Siren:
>one hears your voice:
>from out the Conch Shell:
>shall we meet, then?

68. ABANDONED: HYMN TO JEALOUSY

Abandoned by you:
the fortune-teller said it!
Jealousy blossoms ...

69. TOO COOL FOR SCHOOL

Motorcycle Zen:
you must be: too Cool for School;
a Cig in your Hand ...

70. MEDUSA GAZE: KISS OF THE RAZOR BLADE

I

> Lover, who one worships:
> flit one but a glance:
> shock! Horror! Gasp!
> The sour lover: leers at one!

II

> Most foul a look upon:
> a face that once comforted one:
> Medusa Gaze! Crumbling heart:
> one's world caves in!

III

> One pleas here for clemency:
> where none shall be found:
> refuse one a kiss, lover?
> One will love, then, a razor blade!

IV

>Apparent sadness:
>a certain morose melancholy:
>but nevermore your pet project:
>kissed to death by the razor blade!

71. BANAL SOULS

Who loathes Banal Souls?
Those whom have still a hunger:
for delicacies ...

72. SET SAIL: MALAISE

When it first set sail:
we all knew it would sink;
sure enough: it did!

73. SATURNINE LOVER: INCUBATED SOUL

I

One is a Saturnine lover:
sat down, lost in Soul:
sipping milkshakes of lead:
in a maudlin sort of way!

II

One has had enough lead:
one would be better off dead:
let us walk into the flames:
with or without you: one goes!

III

Treading, now, into the fire:
as usual, one suffers alone:
how is the weather over yonder?
One's Soul incubates: Fahrenheit 3000°.

74. NECROMANCER: CAPITALIST

Necromancy works:
just ask your boss: after you
die: you will be back!

75. ATONEMENT: MIAMI BLEACH

Wash away one's Sins:
bathing in Miami Bleach:
under the Hot Sun ...

76. PRIED OPEN CLAM: ROSE GOLDEN SARCOPHAGUS: RAGDOLL TOY

I

Disaster: a pried open clam:
no pearl nests in your Soul!

II

Rose golden sarcophagus:
reveal to us your dreary contents!

III

A ragdoll, mummified:
it finally had its Soul broken ...

IV

Killed off by a child during play:
now the kid has a new favorite toy!

77. ONE'S MISS ANGELINE

One often wonders:
when will the Void come for her:
one's Miss Angeline?

78. WORLD'S SHORTEST NOVEL

Love was to be had:
and Lovers were to be glad:
but the Goon went Mad.

79. PARROT OF DOOM: DARK INSTRUCTIONS

I

Relative died: inherited a Parrot:
fluently can it speak!

II

Pull back the cage drape:
will it be awake to squawk?

III

Come closer: it demands:
it says: give up on your Soul!

IV

Dread rules the day: imbibe:
allow the Nothing to claim your Soul!

V

> Then the Parrot turned: danced:
> died: and sunk into the Nothing ...

80. BROOKLYN BANSHEE

Who wails in the Night?
From Dumbo to Williamsburg?
The Brooklyn Banshee ...

81. SINS OF THE FLESH

Few pursue the Dark:
exploring Sins of the Flesh:
drumbeats of the Soul ...

82. BATHTUB MAELSTROM: OASIS IN THE SEWER

I

Warm sud bubbles:
enveloped in Sin:
stopper in the drain:
foot dislodges suction cup!

II

Swift alteration of scene:
Rubber Ducky drifts away:
down the drain: gone!
Now you slip down the Pipe!

III

Maelstrom: Rip Tide:
gentle pull of the Water:
one floats like a sea turtle:
an Oasis in the Sewer!

83. FORCES OF ASSHOLEDOM

Around the Soul they ...
the Forces of Assholedom ...
Malaise one the most!

84. BALM REQUESTED: BALM DENIED

May one have a balm?
If you can spare one, that is ...
No? One has kept tabs!

85. MORAL TAX EVASION:
DEFENSE OF THE PIOUS SIN

I

> Judgment comes: all Souls must
> pay their debts: bring them forward!

II

> Tax of Souls: pay your dues!
> But: one refuses to pay!

III

> Toward one's defense:
> one has committed Pious Sin!

IV

> Let this Soul pass on by:
> no toll is needed from a Pious Sinner!

86. ONLY TIME MAY TELL

Will one stay or go?
You know how one gets Malaised ...
Only time may tell!

87. BEDWETTING SOUL: BLEACH IS A CURE-ALL

Oh, Bedwetting Soul:
drowned in Whiskey and Urine:
Bleach is a cure-all!

88. SOUL CRATERS: OPERAS ON THE MOON

I

Observe the Soul Craters:
nurse procure the tweezers:
remove the shards of glass:
wounds that will never heal ...

II

Akin to the Moon: there
are Craters of the Soul;
land a Lunar Rover:
on the Dark Side of Soul ...

III

Position with the tweezers:
operatic singers ready:
to sing their Souls away:
on the Stage of Depravity!

89. BLUE SKIES AND GOLDEN SUNSHINE

No sight of Malaise;
Blue Skies and Golden Sunshine:
Oops: no: there it is!

90. OCTOPUS: SUCTION CUPS TO THE SOUL

Now under the Sea:
an Octopus beak nearby:
Suction Cups: Soul caught ...

91. DESPERATE SEANCE: MORNING OF THE MOURNING

I

Sugar in the coffee:
cream, too: awake already!

II

This is the morning of the:
mourning: imagine its night!

III

Gone too soon: come back!
Seance room: signs from beyond!

IV

Our beloved reaches out to us:
come into the Void: why wait?

92. WANTON SOULS: HIDE IN THE DARK

Wanton Souls: sad tale:
in the Light: Souls shrivel up;
they Hide in the Dark ...

93. DESIROUS TO DIE

Under the Moonlight:
one bathed: Desirous to Die;
Malaise spread too far ...

94. POP: UP ON A HOT AIR BALLOON

I

> Up: soaring higher, higher:
> Papa: play your lyre!

II

> Who blew up this balloon?
> Suddenly it tremored!

III

> Pop: went the balloon:
> flailing: descending: flaming!

IV

> Not a thing survived the crash:
> except for, of course: the lyre ...

95. SOUL HARPOON: BAD LUCK OPAL

Wore an Opal Ring:
Malaise then harpooned one's Soul:
Opal was to blame!

96. ONE'S TENDER BUTTONS

One's Tender Buttons:
you know the Rules of this Game:
play at your own Risk!

97. HYMN TO GLUTTONY: HYMN TO DECADENCE

I

Lift up a howl to the Moon:
a celebration of Decadence!

II

Everyday is a feast:
deprivation is unknown!

III

Gluttonous Souls:
every need: satiated: downfall!

IV

Almost died, again:
yet one has a hunger!

V

More Souls! More Souls!
Thrown into the melting pot.

VI

Gluttonous roles:
cannibalism of the Soul!

VII

One who knows right from wrong:
knows not the pleasures of Decadence!

98. HOUNDS OF HELL

There are Hounds of Hell:
sniffing out one's scent right now!
Pardon one's Malaise ...

99. SUNFLOWER VERSUS WRECKING BALL

Sunflower versus:
Wrecking Ball: occurs tonight!
Sunflower is crushed ...

100. BARRICADE: BATTERING RAM: SOUL DONS A WHITE FLAG

I

Barricade: beyond it lies:
an Innermost Sanctum of: your Soul;
Privacy is a heresy to some folk:
oh look: they bring a Battering Ram!

II

Held still: wound back:
swung into a collision ...
with your Soul, guarded;
raise again the Siege Ram!

III

Beleaguered: will you surrender?
Their forces have dug trenches:
they seek to unearth all of your Secrets:
Ceasefire: your Soul dons a White Flag!

101. SOUL IN THE TROUGH: HUNGRY HOGS

One's Soul in the Trough;
salivating Hungry Hogs:
you let the Swine out!

102. ALOHA FROM THE VOID

Aloha from the ...
Void; one dons a Hawaiian Shirt:
shelter from Malaise!

103. EASTER CLOTHES: WOODCHIPPER OF SOULS: JIGSAW PUZZLE

I

Been hearing threats about it:
for years: then you say:
it is time: one gathers oneself:
one puts on one's Easter Clothes!

II

Will there be ectoplasm:
when the ritual occurs —
when you take one's Soul:
and cast it into the Woodchipper?

III

One's Soul is now in pieces:
even if you cared to:
would you put together again:
this Jigsaw Puzzle that you caused?

104. METHINKS ONE LOVES YOU

Malaise: one falters;
through the darkness you lead one:
hand-clasped for dear life!

105. BORE SOME MORE: INCREASED ENNUI

Well respected bore:
how about you bore some more?
Increase one's Ennui!

106. SHOCK TREATMENT: SOUL TRANSFUSION: CURE FOR BANALITY

I

> Young ones grow still:
> malaise conquers Souls!

II

> Round up the adults:
> they suffer from banality the most!

III

> Shock treatment may work:
> hook up their Souls to the current!

IV

> Buzz! They remain the Living Dead!
> Bah: a last resort: Soul Transfusion!

V

Due to donor Souls, the bland:
get a second chance at Life!

107. YOUR LEGS: A DECEPTIVE TRAP

Trying to resist:
your legs: a Deceptive Trap:
shelter from Malaise ...

108. FORTUNE COOKIE: THE BLACK SPOT

Opened the cookie:
profound Malaise: The Black Spot:
Say your good-byes, Soul!

109. HALL OF MIRRORS: MALAISE

I

An adrenaline shot to the Soul:
one's Punishment: Reflection!

II

One sees all of the years:
all of one's loves: one's Temptations!

III

One looks into a Mirror:
one sees one's own Damnation!

IV

Lover whom one has seen die:
Comfort one while you can!

V

Hall of Mirrors, reveal:
but one more grim reality!

VI

In the Mirror: your Childhood:
how many years ago! Malaise!

110. LAUGHING GAS

Hook oneself up now:
Laughing Gas functions as balm:
for which Wound? Malaise!

111. ALL ROADS LEAD TO HELL

Heard of the Good News?
Go Listen to the Preacher Man:
All Roads Lead to Hell!

112. BABY'S FIRST WORD: TEQUILA

I

Baby!
Over there:
next to the:
Lady!

II

Juxtaposition:
the Baby:
next to the:
Lady!

III

One so fresh!
Natal innocence!
Next to the:
alcoholic Lady!

IV

Baby's first word:
shocked not the Lady:
Tequila; already:
Baby is malaised!

V

Warm: cradled;
while Lady has:
not been cuddled:
in thirteen years!

VI

Baby: so young:
with a future ahead:
Lady craves renewal:
perhaps a new life!

VII

Lady broke down:
Baby this, Baby that:
Baby who has everything!
Lady who has nothing!

VIII

Baby demands more:
Lady has enough:
Baby begins to cry:
Lady lies down: dies ...

www.ingramcontent.com/pod-product-compliance
Lightning Source LLC
Chambersburg PA
CBHW061656040426
42446CB00010B/1771